KU-094-269

JOKE LOCKER

make believe ideas

Copyright © 2018

make believe ideas ltd

The Wilderness, Berkhamsted, Hertfordshire, HP4 2AZ, UK.

All rights reserved. No part of this publication may be reproduced,
stored in a retrieval system, or transmitted in any form or by any means,
electronic, mechanical, photocopying, recording, or otherwise, without
the prior written permission of the copyright owner.

Recommended for children aged 6 and over.

www.makebelieveideas.com

Illustrated by Pedro Demetriou, Stuart Lynch & Sarah Vince.

ARE YOU READY TO UNLOCK A **MEGA** JOKE SESSION?

This book is jam-packed with every kind of joke you can imagine! You'll find all the best knock-knock jokes, doctor-doctor ticklers, animal gags and funny messages.

There's also space to record any other side-splitters you hear along the way, as well as instructions for writing your own jokes.

Prepare to **never** be bored again!

WARNING: This book is not suitable for people who lack a sense of humour!

Why did the snake go to school?

To study hisstory!

Why are noses always putting their hands up?

Because they love to be picked!

Why did the toilet see the doctor?

Because it felt a little FLUSHED!

Why did the brainiac eat her homework?

Because she thought it was a piece of cake!

Why did the fool cut a hole in his umbrella?

So he could see when it stopped raining!

Why did the broom get married so fast?
Because she was swept off her feet!

Why didn't the snowman go to the disco?
Because he had tickets to the snow ball!

Why did the tomato blush?
Because he saw the salad dressing!

Why did the man take a clock on the plane?
He wanted to see time fly!

Why did the monster eat the torch?
He wanted a light snack!

Why did the jelly wobble?

Because he saw the milk shake!

Why did the lift visit the doctor?

Because it came down with a cold!

Why did the music-loving boy stick a shoe to his ear?

Because he liked SOUL music!

Why did the fool sit on a clock?

He was told to work overtime!

Why did the fool hang his phone from the ceiling?

Because he was told it was a mobile!

Why did the vegetable house need a new roof?

Because it was full of leeks!

Why did the cookie go to the hospital?

Because it felt crumby!

Why did the light bulb fail its exams?

It wasn't very bright!

Why did the moon burp?

Because it was full!

Why did the teacher wear dark glasses?

Because her students were too bright!

Why did the computer feel sick?
It had too many chips!

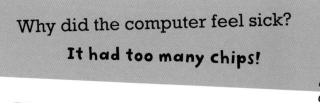

Why did the fungus want a bigger house?
He didn't have mushroom!

Why did the computer hide his cheese?
So the mouse wouldn't eat it!

Why did the bean run away from the farm?
The farmer was picking on him!

Why did the apartment
building become a library?
**Because it had
so many stories!**

What did the kettle say when the saucepan lost his temper?

Just SIMMER down!

What did the dice say when the cards refused to shuffle?

I'll DEAL with you later!

How do you stop your phone battery from running out?

Hide its trainers!

What did the ocean say to the lifeguard?

Nothing, it just waved!

Have you seen the new onion website?

Yes, it's a SITE for sore eyes!

Which vampire lives in a kitchen drawer?

Count SPATULA!

Why are noses with colds super fit?

Because they're always running!

Why was the meatball tired?

Because it was pasta its bedtime!

YAWN!

What kind of vegetables
do you find in the gym?

Muscle sprouts!

What goes HA! HA! BONK!

A man laughing his head off!

OOPS!

What has teeth but cannot eat?

A zip!

How do you make a toilet roll?

Push it down a hill!

What did the sun say to the cloud when he went on holiday?

You'll be MIST!

What do you get if you put your pen in the freezer?

Iced ink?

Well, yes, you do stink, but that's not the answer!

Where's the best place to make noise online?

The DIN-ternet!

Why was the shirt sad?

Because the jeans were blue!

When should you never suck your food?

Chewsday!

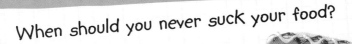

sniff!

Why was the skeleton feeling lonely?

Because he had NO BODY to play with!

What do elves do after school?

Their gnomework!

How do fishermen catch virtual fish?
Online!

Why are scarves bad at sports?
Because they prefer to hang around!

When's the best time to chop down a tree?
Sep-timber!

Which famous sea creature never tidies its room?
The Loch Mess Monster!

What did Mr Volcano say to Mrs Volcano when they got married?
I lava you!

Which sweet treat makes lots of mistakes?

D'oh-nuts!

What did the curtains say to the window?

We've got you covered!

How does the sea wear its hair?

Wavy!

What sound did the grape make when it got squashed?

A little wine!

What type of ice cream does Frankenstein eat?

Cookies 'n' scream!

What do sea monsters eat at parties?

Ships 'n' dip!

Why didn't the artist
leave his bedroom?

**Because he liked
drawing curtains!**

Where do astronauts keep their sandwiches?

In a launch box!

What lives at the bottom
of the sea and shakes?

A nervous wreck!

What's green and refuses
to join in games?

The incredible sulk!

Did you hear about the plumber
who couldn't mend pipes?

His business went down the drain!

Did you hear about the angry man
who mistook his soap for cheese?

He was foaming at the mouth!

Where does the President of the
United States keep his armies?

Up his sleevies!

Why do pirates keep soap under their hats?

To help them wash ashore!

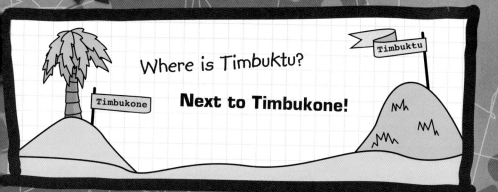

Where is Timbuktu?

Next to Timbukone!

Timbuktu

Timbukone

What did the books say when they couldn't agree?

We're just not on the same page!

What do you get if you have two running taps?

A race!

What goes up and down but never moves?

A flight of stairs!

Which worms have spines?

Bookworms!

BIG BOOK
OF INSECTS
BY KAT A. PILLAR

Which footwear will make you jump?

Boo-ts!

Did you hear about the garden centre full of overgrown trees?

They had to hire a branch manager!

How do snowmen get to work?

On bICICLES!

Why do monsters eat metal pins?

It's their staple diet!

Why couldn't the doctor see her patients?

Because she'd lost her glasses!

How do you know when it's been raining cats and dogs?

The ground is covered in poodles!

What's a cow's favourite dance?

The moo-nwalk!

What do you call a man with a car on his head?

Jack!

Did you hear about the woman who lived next to a wall?

She broke her ladder and never got over it!

Why did the man throw away his paper trousers?

Because they looked tearable!

Why are hairdressers never late for work?

Because they know all the shortcuts!

What did the rockstar do when he locked himself out?

He sang until he found the right key!

Which vegetables will you find on a clothes hanger?

Jacket potatoes!

How do you know if a train is eating gum?

Because you can hear it chew, chew, chew!

Why were the company directors yawning?

They were having a BORED meeting!

When is the best time to visit the dentist?

Tooth hurty!

FUNNY MESSAGES

There's going to be a storm!

Gustov Wynd

I'd recommend this book.

Paige Turner

Wait here for me!

Isa Cumming

The weather's terrible!

Reyna Lott

What's that noise?

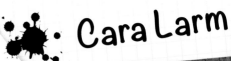

Cara Larm

Can you touch your toes?

Ben Dover

I borrowed your calculator.

Adam Upp

You won a prize!

Anita Ward

I'll meet you at the cinema.

Hugo First

I have a complaint!

Mona Lott

What's a fisherman's favourite musical instrument?

The cast-a-nets!

What's the best snack to eat on a roller-coaster?

F-RISE and dip!

How did the gnome get indigestion?

By goblin his food!

How did the tap dancer break his leg?

He fell in the sink!

Where do barbers keep their money?

In shaving accounts!

Why doesn't gravity have many friends?

Because it brings everyone down!

Why are mushrooms always
invited to parties?

Because they are fun-guys!

What's green and sniffs?

A cucumber with a cold!

How did the cyclist puncture his tyre?

He drove over a fork in the road!

What's red and hairy and goes up and down?

A raspberry in a lift!

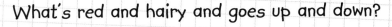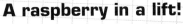

What lives underground and uses bad language?

Crude oil!

Why do fleas never pay train fares?

They prefer itch-hiking!

Did you hear about the scientist
who broke the laws of gravity?

He got a suspended sentence!

Did you hear about the scouts'
chess tournament?

It was in tents!

Did you hear about the man
with size 18 boots?

Finding shoes was no small feet!

What's the longest word in the world?

Smile, because there's a mile after the S!

Waitress, will my spaghetti be long?

**Yes, sir. Would you like me
to cut it up for you?**

Did you hear about the car that couldn't turn left?

It was all right in the end!

What's a pirate's favourite letter?

Arrrr!

Did you hear about the chef who
was crazy for pastries?

She was a dough-nut!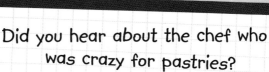

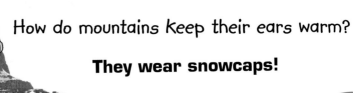

How do mountains keep their ears warm?

They wear snowcaps!

What do you say when you meet
a three-headed alien?

Hello!   Hello!   Hello!

Why should you always wear
glasses for maths?

Because they improve di-vision! $6 \div 2 = 3$

Why is a calculator a faithful friend?

Because you can always count on it!

What do you call an
alien with no name?

Nothing!

What did cavemen use to cut down trees?

Dino-SAWS!

Which snack tastes best on a ghost train?

I scream!

Why was the computer full of holes?

Someone had taken bytes out of it!

What has four legs but can't walk?

A table!

What do you call a cheese that's not yours?

Nacho cheese!

Why couldn't the teddy bear eat any cake?

Because it was stuffed!

Which letters are not in the alphabet?

The ones in the post!

What did the football say to the goalkeeper?

I get a kick out of you!

What should you say when you meet a steep rock face?

Hi, Cliff!

What do you call a man with leaves in his boots?

Russell!

What do you call fake pasta?

Mockeroni!

What did the cola do after knitting a scarf?

Soda dress!

What do you call a fairy who has fallen in manure?

Stinkerbell!

Why can't you order a clownfish in a restaurant?

Because it tastes funny!

How do you make a hotdog stand?

Hide its chair!

What's orange and sounds like a parrot?

A carrot!

What do clouds wear under their jeans?

Thunderpants!

What's the best way to get a fish online?

Catch it Internet!

What do elves learn at school?

The elf-abet!

When did the pencil stop talking?

When it got to the point!

How much does it cost to pierce a pirate's ear?

A buccaneer!

Why do dentists never lie?

Because they always tell the tooth!

What's Tarzan's favourite lesson?

Hippopot-a-maths!

What has a lot of heads and tails but no body?

A pocket full of change!

FUNNY MESSAGES

Meet me by the river.

Brook Lynne Bridge

It doesn't add up!

Cal Culator

I've gone for a haircut.

Hedda Hare

Hip, hip!

Hugh Ray

Do you want salad for dinner?

May O'Nays

Cut the grass!

Lorna Mower

Looks fishy
to me ...

Anne Chovie

I really can't be
bothered.

Ariel Hassle

Would you like
to join the
orchestra?

Clara Nett

Get your
hair cut!

Si de Burns

The police are after me!

Robyn Banks

What did he say?

Candy B. Hurd

Got to run or I'll miss my bus!

Nick Ovtime

Meet you on the top floor.

Ella Vader

What would you like for lunch?

Chi Spurger

Meet you at the zoo.
Al E. Gaytor
Get off the sofa!
Stan Dupp
Help! I can't get out!
Doris Shutt
Stand up straight!
Denise R. Bent
Turn the music down!
Max E. Mumm

Why was the chick's phone confiscated?

Because he wouldn't stop tweeting!

Why was the sheep sent to its room?

Because it had been baa-ed!

How do bees style their hair?

With honeycombs!

Where do kittens play?

A-mews-ment parks!

What do you call a cow eating grass?

A lawn mooer!

If seagulls fly over the sea, what flies over the bay?

Bay-gulls!

Why don't cats like the colour green?

Because they prefer purr-ple!

What do elephants wear to the beach?

Swimming trunks!

What type of dog works in a hair salon?

A shampoodle!

Why don't grasshoppers cry?

Because they're always hoppy!

Doctor, Doctor, I think I'm a baby cod!

Sounds a little fishy to me!

Doctor, Doctor, I think I'm a submarine!

You're clearly out of your depth!

Doctor, Doctor, I think I'm a moth!

Move out of the light!

Doctor, Doctor, I think I'm a yo-yo!

How do you feel?

Sometimes I'm up and sometimes I'm down!

Doctor, Doctor, my nose is 11 inches long!

Come back if it grows into a foot!

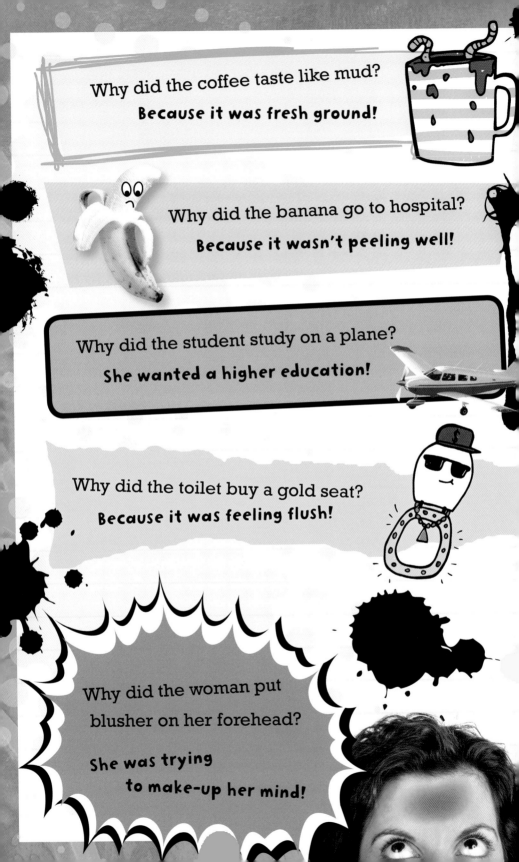

Why did the coffee taste like mud?
Because it was fresh ground!

Why did the banana go to hospital?
Because it wasn't peeling well!

Why did the student study on a plane?
She wanted a higher education!

Why did the toilet buy a gold seat?
Because it was feeling flush!

Why did the woman put blusher on her forehead?
She was trying to make-up her mind!

Why did the policeman refuse to get out of bed?

He wanted to work undercover!

Why did the eyes give up teaching?

Because they only had two pupils!

Why did the car refuse to move?

Because its wheels were tyre-d!

Why didn't the knife trust the spoon?

Because the spoon kept stirring things up!

Why did the fool put bowls of milk and water in his garden?

He heard it was going to rain cats and dogs!

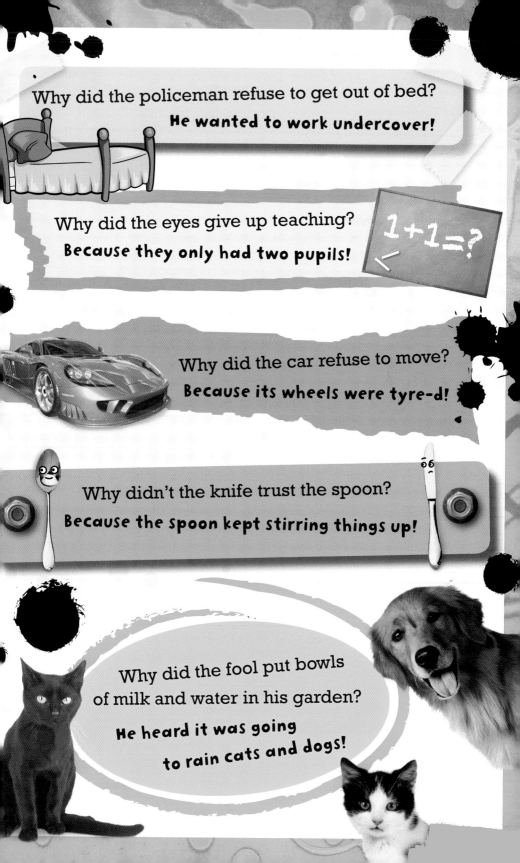

Why did the grey pebble wear bright purple trousers?

He wanted to be a little bolder!

Why did the picture go to jail?

Because it was framed!

Why didn't anyone eat the overripe banana?

Because it wasn't a-peeling!

Why did the socks sit in the fruit bowl?

They were told they were a pear!

Why did the lady have her hair in a bun?

Because she'd eaten all her burgers!

Why did the boy keep
his headphones in the fridge?

Because he liked cool music!

Why did the rose go to university?

She was a budding genius!

Why did the flea lose the singing contest?

Because he wasn't up to scratch!

Why did the apple run away?

Because the banana split!

Why did the boy cover his hands in fertiliser?

He was trying to grow palm trees!

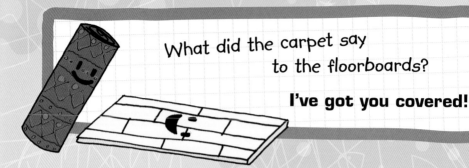

What did the carpet say to the floorboards?

I've got you covered!

Why do golfers carry spare socks?

In case they get a hole in one!

Why are football players messy eaters?

Because they are always dribbling!

Why was the belt arrested?

For holding up the trousers!

How many ears do cowboys have?

Three: a left ear, a right ear and a wild frontier!

Where do American footballers eat Thanksgiving dinner?

The supper bowl!

What's yellow and sneezes?

A lemon with a cold!

How do sports stars stay cool?

They sit next to their fans!

Why did the girl sit on the ladder to sing?

She wanted to hit the high notes!

How did the lamp feel when its *bulb* burnt out?

De-lighted!

What did the tree say
to the boulder?

You rock!

Why is the ocean so messy?

**Because the fish never
make the seabed!**

What did the sand say when
the sea asked for a date?

Shore!

How do you make a milkshake?

Tell it a scary story!

Which part of a tree makes cats jump?

The bark!

How do you make a cheese puff?

Chase it round the supermarket!

What did the tree say when it was feeling sad?

Just leaf me alone!

What's the ocean's favourite game?

Tide and seek!

Why did the banana miss school?

It was peeling bad!

Why are trees always ready for a swim?

Because they are never without their trunks!

Why was Cinderella bad at sports?

She was always running from the ball!

Why do babies make good basketball players?

Because they are good at dribbling!

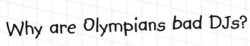

Why are Olympians bad DJs?

Because they are always breaking records!

Why was the singer locked out of her house?

She couldn't find the right key!

Who can jump higher than the Empire State Building?

Everyone – the Empire State Building can't jump!

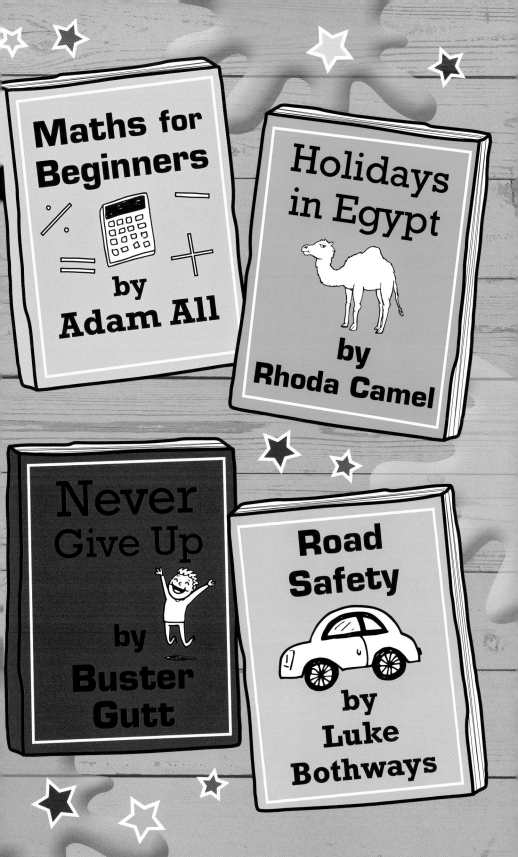

How do rabbits go on holiday?

By hare-plane!

What do you call a girl with a frog on her head?

Lily!

Why are elephants bad dancers?

Because they have two left feet!

What do you call a bear that's missing an ear?

B!

What do you call cows with a fit of the giggles?

Laughing stock!

What's a sheep's favourite snack?
A baa of chocolate!

Na-na-na-na!

What do you get if you cross a yellow fruit with a fire engine?
A bana-na-na-na-na-na-na!

What's a cat's favourite dessert?
Mice cream!

Why don't people like working in bakeries?
Because they're crumby places!

Which bagel topping loves riding roller-coasters?
Scream cheese!

How do farmers mend their sleeves?

With cabbage patches!

What do lazy bakers do?

Nothing, they just loaf around!

Why did the baker have to sell his business?

Because he ran out of dough!

What did the cheese say to the knife?

I've never felt grater!

Which cups are impossible to drink from?

Hiccups!

How do you find a lost train?

Follow its tracks!

Did you hear about the man who sold tall yachts?

His sails went through the roof!

Where should you take a sick ship?

The doc!

Why did the bat miss the train?

He was hanging around too long!

What's the best way to travel underwater?

By octobus!

What do you call pigs who won't let you pass?

Road hogs!

How do you make a car disappear?

Turn it into a side street!

Where do cars like to go for a swim?

The carpool!

What type of driver doesn't need a licence?

A screwdriver!

Why is an old car like a baby?

They both have a rattle!

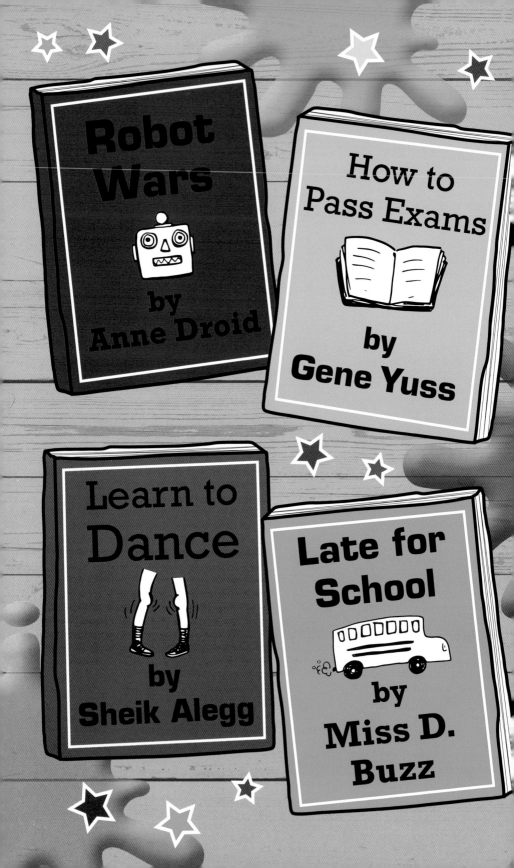

Why do you never meet rich hens?

Because they'll work for chicken feed!

Which basketball players can jump higher than the hoop?
All of them – hoops can't jump!

Which pets love bowling?

Alley cats!

Why did the pancake chef sign up for baseball?

He made a good batter!

Which dogs are good at combat sports?

Boxers!

What did the socks say to the hat?

You go on ahead; we'll go on foot!

Which U.S. state has the best-dressed football players?

New Jersey!

What's the hardest thing about skydiving?

The ground!

Why did the football quit sport?

It was tired of being kicked around!

Why was the basketball court so wet?

Because it had been dribbled all over!

What kind of rabbits own yachts?

Millionhares!

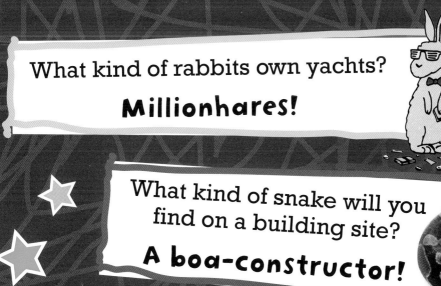

What kind of snake will you find on a building site?

A boa-constructor!

Why didn't the mermaid like the shrimp?

Because it was so shellfish!

When are most chimps born?

Ape-ril!

What do you call a bear caught in the rain?

Drizzly!

What do you get if you cross a dog with an aeroplane?

A jet-setter!

Girl to her mum: I've been cycling to school for three weeks now!

Mum to her daughter: Oh dear, I didn't think it would take that long!

Did you hear about the police investigation into stolen luggage?

It's a very interesting case!

How do snake charmers keep their windscreens clean?

With windscreen vipers!

Why did the farmer's boat sink?

Because it was filled with leeks!

What's big and scary and has one wheel?

A monster on a unicycle!

What's the laziest machine on a building site?

The bull-dozer!

Z Z Z

Which type of market should you never take a dog to?

A flea market!

Which ships have lots of students on board?

Scholarships!

Why was the dinosaur?

Because it bumped its head!

Why did the snowman go to the vegetable shop?

He wanted to pick his nose!

What type of music do elves listen to at the North Pole?

Wrap music!

Which school supplies should always be obeyed?

Rulers!

Why are protractors smart?

Because they have 180 degrees.

How do bees get to school?

They take the school buzz!

What's a runner's favourite school subject?

Jog-raphy!

Why is Florida full of locks?

Because of all the Keys!

Which islands do sheep like best?

The Baa-hamas!

Why didn't the skeleton want to go skydiving?

Because he didn't have the guts!

Why do fish get good marks?

Because they stay in schools!

What do planets like to listen to on the radio?
Nep-tunes!

Why did the boy go outside with his rucksack open?
He was hoping for some change in the weather!

Why are trees friendlier than they look?
Because their bark is worse than their bite!

Which plants have mouths?
Tulips!

What gets bigger the more you take away from it?
A hole in the ground!

What do you call handful of sand?

Palm Beach!

What's the scariest kind of horse?

A night-mare!

Why did the man get rid of his wooden car?

Because it wooden go!

Why did the moon skip dessert?

Because it was full!

What did the mother worm say to her son?

Where in earth have you been?!

Why do grapes have big families?
Because they love raisin kids!

Why was the strawberry late for work?
It was stuck in a jam!

When do astronauts have their sandwiches?
At launch time!

Which books are like fruitcakes?
History books, because they're full of dates!

What did the milk say when the cream turned sour?
Yogurt to be kidding!

Why did the doughnut visit the dentist?

It needed a filling!

Why did the boy put his cake in the freezer?

Because he was trying to ice it!

What did the doctor say to the man with carrots in his ears?

You're not eating properly!

What's brown and hairy and sits by the pool?

A coconut on holiday!

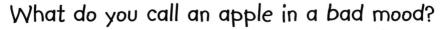

What do you call an apple in a bad mood?

A crab apple!

Hmmm, hmmm, hmmm!

Why was the car engine humming?

Because it didn't know the words!

When can a tortoise go as fast as a bus?

When it's sitting on a bus seat!

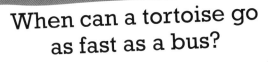

Do trains have eyes?

No, but they do have engine-ears!

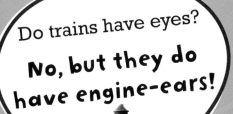

Why was the train never behind schedule?

Because it was always on track!

Why did the dinosaur go to the garage?

His car had a flat tyre-annosaurus!

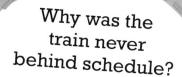

Which motorbikes are the most fun to ride?

Yamaha-ha-has!

Ha-ha-ha!

Why did the bike keep falling over?

Because it was two tyred!

What do metal-eating monsters eat for breakfast?

Chew-chew trains!

The croak's on me!

What did the driver say to the hitchhiking frog?

Hop in!

What do you call a train with the flu?

A-choo-choo train!

A-choo-choo!

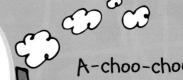

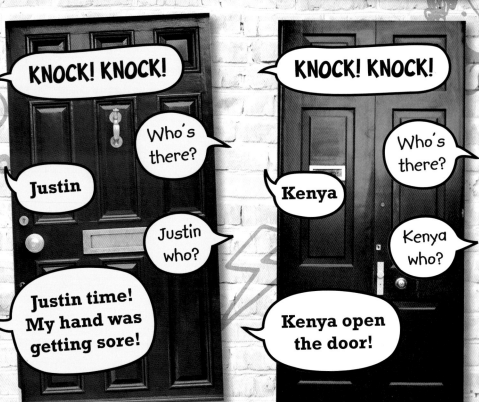

Why did the spider buy a laptop?
To build a website!

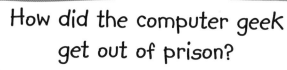

How did the computer geek
get out of prison?
He pushed escape!

e s c

Why was the
computer late
for work?

**It had a
hard drive!**

Why did the
computer go to
the restaurant?

**It wanted a
byte to eat!**

Why do keyboards
take so long to put
on their shirts?

**Because they
have so many
buttons!**

What do monsters put on their laptops?

Scream savers!

Where did the computer geek kick her ball?

Internet!

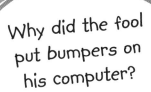

Why did the fool put bumpers on his computer?

He was afraid it might crash!

Why shouldn't you leave cheese on your computer?

Because the mouse might eat it!

Which search engine do slime monsters use?

Gooo-gle!

How to be Clever
by
Noah Tall

Petrol Station
Management
by
Phil McCarup

Building Your Own Home
by
Isadore There

Extreme Workouts
by
A. King

Lovely Views
by
Cliff Topp

Barbecue Ribs
by
Nora Bone

How to be a Comedian
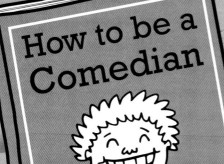
by
Joe King

Stormy Weather

by
Augusta Wind

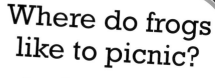

Where do frogs like to picnic?

Under croak trees!

Which chickens tell the best jokes?

Comedi-hens!

Why did the rabbit move into a flat?

She was bored of the hole thing!

How long should a giraffe's legs be?

Long enough to reach the ground!

What type of dog did the magician buy?

A labra-cadabra!

Which circus performers have wings?
Acro-bats!

What kind of films do rabbits like?
Ones with hoppy endings!

How do snails settle arguments?
They slug it out!

Why do cats keep away from trees?
Because they're afraid of their bark!

What did the cat say when it bumped its head?
Me-OW!

When are hamburger chefs busiest?
On fry-day!

Why did the Italian chef throw away his spaghetti?
Because it was pasta its best!

Why did the barber quit his job?
He couldn't cut it!

Why did the waitress quit her job in space?
Because the restaurant had no atmosphere!

Which Star Wars character loves fishing?
Darth Wader!

What do you say to a thirsty dinosaur?
Tea, Rex?

Why did the maze designer quit his job?
He kept getting lost in his work!

What did the baker give his wife on Valentine's Day?
Flours!

What did the detective say to his new boss?
Policed to meet you!

Why did the mattress become a spy?
It wanted to be undercover!

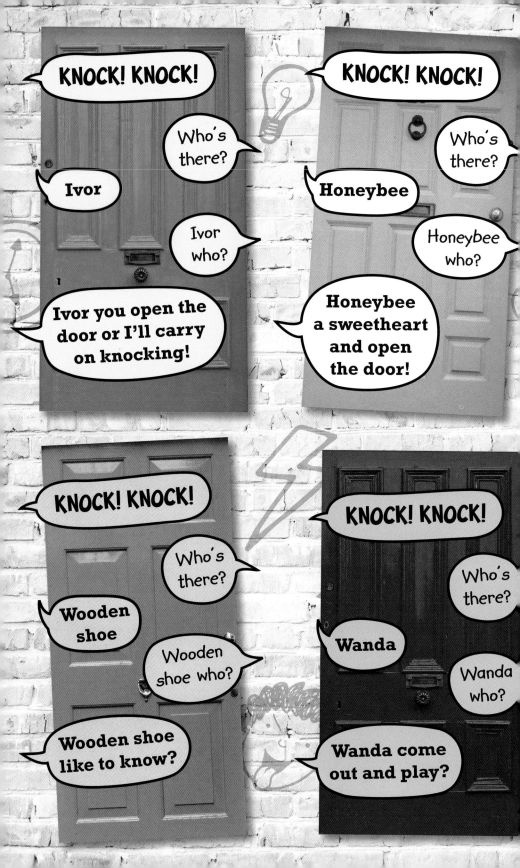

Which sport is often found
in back gardens?

Fencing!

Where do badminton players
go to become famous?

Volleywood!

 VOLLEYWOOD

Which insects
can't catch?

Fumble bees!

Why don't fish
play tennis?

**Because they
don't want to be
caught in the net!**

Which sport
do birds play
in winter?

Ice hawkey!

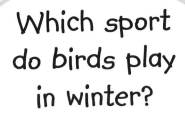

Why was Cinderella's football team always losing?
Because it had a pumpkin for a coach!

Which sport is the loudest?
Tennis, because of the racket!

What's always served but never eaten?
A tennis ball!

What is a football player's least favourite drink?
Penal tea!

What is a hairdresser's favourite winter sport?
Curling!

What's the easiest way to get straight A's?
Use a ruler!

Did you hear the one about the girl who left her pencil sharpener at home?
She couldn't see the point!

What's the first lesson at gardening school?
Weeding and writing!

Why was the maths exam worrying?
Because it had so many problems!

Why did the student walk to school on stilts?
Because she wanted a higher education!

Where do pirates go on holiday?

Arrr-gentina!

What's the best way to get to school?

On the sylla-bus!

Why did the music teacher bring a ladder to class?

So her students could reach the high notes!

Why do libraries need lifts?

Because they have so many stories!

What do you learn first at baseball school?

The alpha-bat!

What do trees wear on the beach?

Swimming trunks!

What's an octopus's favourite playground ride?

The sea-saw!

How do you know if a farmer is good at his job?

He'll be out standing in his field!

How can you tell if the ocean's in a good mood?

It waves!

What happens if you slip on a mountain?

You hit rock bottom!

What did the bee say to the sunflower?

Hi, Honey!

What do you give a lemon tree with a broken branch?

Lemon aid!

What did the beaver say to the log?

It's good to get to gnaw you!

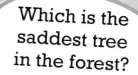

Which is the saddest tree in the forest?

The weeping willow!

What's smartly dressed and growls on your lawn?

A dandy lion!

What do you call a monster wearing earphones?

Anything — he can't hear you!

Where do European hamsters live?

Hamsterdam!

What do you call a cow on a roller-coaster?

A milk shake!

Why are bulls louder than cars?

Because they have two horns!

How are crimes solved in swamps?

By investi-gators!

Where do sheep go for haircuts?

The baa-bers!

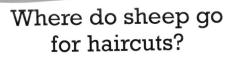

Which dogs always know the time?

Watch dogs!

Why do dragons rest during the day?

So they are ready to fight knights!

How do you find a pesky mosquito?

Start from scratch!

What's a cat's favourite type of show?

A mew-sical!

Old Furniture
by
Ann Teak

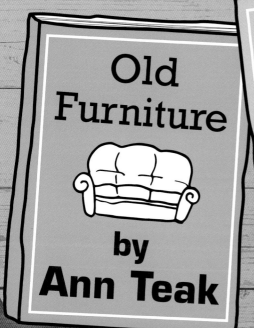

Window Dressings
by
Annette Curtain

My Cow Escaped!
by
Gay Topen

Tasty Breakfasts
by
Egan Bacon

What's the best way to prepare dinner in space?

Planet!

What do you get if you cross a dog with a sausage?

Pupperoni!

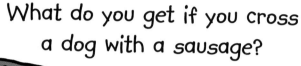

Why did the mouse take a bath?

So it would be squeaky clean!

What's the best day to eat ice cream?

Sundae!

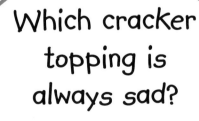

Which cracker topping is always sad?

Blue cheese!

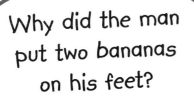

Why did the man put two bananas on his feet?

Because he wanted a pair of slippers!

Why do bananas keep out of the sun?
Because they peel easily!

Why did the orange go to the petrol station?
Because it ran out of juice!

Why did the Italian meal go to Vegas?
For a pizza the action!

Which fruit can mend your shower?
Plum-ers!

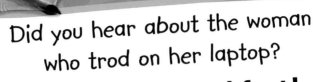

Did you hear about the woman who trod on her laptop?

She got webbed feet!

Why was the computer geek's house cold?

Because he never closed Windows!

Did you hear about the boy who was on his computer all night?

He'd have been a lot more comfortable in bed!

Why is shopping on the Internet dangerous?

Because your trolley might fall off the computer!

How did the computers afford to buy a gift?

They all chipped in!

What did the fool do when his screen froze?

He put it in the microwave!

How do lumberjacks start their computers?

They log in!

Why did the cat get bored of computing?

Because it couldn't scare the mouse!

How do hungry computers eat their lunch?

With mega bites!

Why are flies scared of computers?

They don't want to get caught in the web!

Why didn't the boy take the bus to school?

It was too big to fit through the door!

How do pilots like their bagels?

Plane!

Why couldn't the duck see where he was going?

Because his windscreen was quacked!

Why do train guards look so tall?

Because they wear platform shoes!

Why was the train found guilty?

Because it had a clear loco-motive!

Why was the railway driver bad at his job?

Because he wasn't trained!

What do you call a jumbo jet going the wrong way?

An error-plane!

Why would Peter Pan make a bad pilot?

Because he would Neverland!

Why are tyres so expensive?

Because of inflation!

Why was the petrol angry with the truck?

Because it took him for a fuel!

Why was the boy's assignment wet?

It was below C level!

Why did the builder flunk
his roof-tiling class?

Because it was over his head!

Why was the teacher
angry with the echo?

**It kept
answering back!**

Why did the teacher
move his class to
a penthouse?

**Because he wanted to
work in a high school!**

Why did the teacher
write on the window?

**So her lessons
would be clear!**

Why did the lumberjack fail his exams?

Because he was stumped!

Why did the teacher find it hard to concentrate?

Because she couldn't control her pupils!

What do you call a boy with an encyclopedia in his back pocket?

Smarty pants!

What stays in one place but travels all over the world?

A postage stamp!

Which month is the shortest?

May, because it's only got three letters!

LAUGHTER LAB

This section gives you the silly science behind four classic jokes. Find out how they're made, and then create some of your own.

CLASSIC GAG No. 1

I say, my dog's got no nose!

How does he smell?

Terrible!

It's the unexpected answer that makes this joke truly special. The obvious, unfunny conversation would go something like this . . .

I say, my dog's got no nose!

How does he smell?

He can't because he hasn't got a nose.

Not funny. It's the two meanings of "smell" that make this gag funny: It's not how the dog can smell (obvious), but what he smells like (comedy gold).

You can make this joke your own by changing the animal and rewording the punchline. *For example:*

. . . Like a wrestler's armpit!

. . . Like last week's cat food!

. . . As bad as your feet!

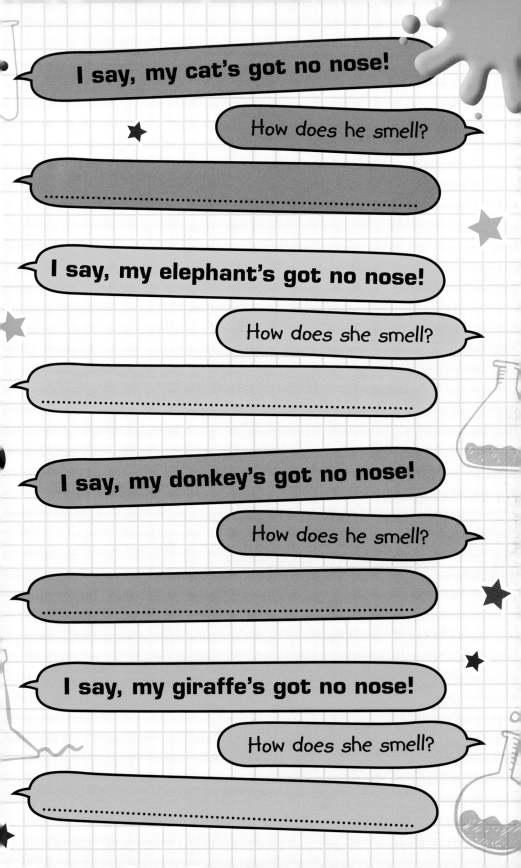

CLASSIC GAG No. 2

Name puns can be an endless source of 5★ jesting. Names that sound like other words can be used to make funny book titles.

How to get rich

BY IONA FORTUNE

For example: "Justin" sounds like "just in", so your book could be called:

The Day I Nearly Missed Dinner
BY JUSTIN TIME

Here's another: "Eileen" sounds like "I lean", so your joke could be . . .

I Could Never Stand Straight
BY EILEEN A. LITTLE

And finally: "Tim Burr" sounds like "timber", so your joke could be . . .

Being a Lumberjack
BY TIM BURR

Wayne Drops = raindrops

Ella Fant = elephant

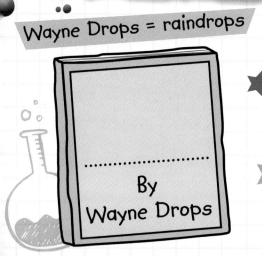

By
Wayne Drops

By Ella
Fant

Everyone loves a good knock-knock joke! The moment of mirth comes from the answer to the question "Who's there?" because the answer is always a pun. In the joke on the door below, "Police" really means "please".

The formula of a basic knock-knock joke looks like this:

Knock! Knock! + Who's there? + *Name* + *Name* who? + Pun = Gag!

KNOCK! KNOCK!

Who's there?

Police

Police who?

Police let me in, it's raining!

Here's an example:

KNOCK! KNOCK!

Who's there?

Clare

Clare who?

Clare the room, I'm coming in!

And another:

KNOCK! KNOCK!

Who's there?

Ida

Ida who?

Ida hoped you'd know it was me!

Why did the chicken cross the road?

To get to the other side!

The basic chicken joke is a non-joke; you expect a witty answer, but instead you get a plain fact. Chicken jokes aren't funny, but they are really annoying, which is almost as good!

Here are three ways to make the chicken joke your own:

1 Swap the chicken for another animal, and think of a funny reason for it to cross the road. Try to include the chicken. *For example:*

Why did the bug cross the road?

He was stuck on the chicken's foot!

2 Give the chicken a different reason to cross. *For example:*

Why did the chicken cross the road?

Because it was easier than crossing the river!

3 Change the road into something else. *For example:*

Why did the chicken cross the beach?

To get to the other sea-side!

Joke Journal

Whenever you hear or create a good joke,
jot it down here so you won't forget it.